Preston Bailey's

FANTASY WEDDINGS

FANTASY WEDDINGS

PRESTON BAILEY

with Beth Decker

Photographs by John Labbé

BULFINCH PRESS

New York • Boston

Bulfinch Press
Time Warner Book Group
1271 Avenue of the Americas
New York, NY 10020
Visit our Web site at www.bulfinchpress.com

First Edition

Library of Congress Cataloging-in-Publication Data
Bailey, Preston.
  Preston Bailey's fantasy weddings / Preston Bailey with Beth Decker ; photographs
by John Labbé.—1st ed.
      p. cm.
  Includes index.
  ISBN 0-8212-2869-2
  1. Weddings—Case studies. 2. Weddings—Pictorial works. 3. Wedding
decorations. I. Decker, Beth. II. Labbé, John. III. Title.

  HQ745.B33 2004
  395.2'2—dc22

                                    2004004555

Designed by Lynne Yeamans/Lync
Photographs on pages 110–119 by Roger Dong

PRINTED IN SINGAPORE

To Peter Azrak

for all his guidance, wisdom, and friendship

Contents

Introduction

fantasy: FANCY; *esp*: the free play of creative imagination

— MERRIAM-WEBSTER'S COLLEGIATE DICTIONARY, ELEVENTH EDITION, 2003

BEGINNING IN CHILDHOOD, A WEDDING DAY IS IMAGINED AS THE PERFECT FANTASY. LITTLE GIRLS DRESS UP AS brides, and even if it's just tying a pillowcase to their heads, suddenly — in their mind's eye — they are glorious princesses, waltzing with their perfect prince as a gossamer veil flows behind them. A sprig of wildflowers picked from the backyard transforms itself into a glorious bouquet, full of the most luscious blooms. Even in fairy tales, the ultimate conclusion of a storybook adventure often ends with the perfect wedding. As we grow into adults,

THIS PINK PINEAPPLE IS THE EPITOME OF FANTASY. ALTHOUGH YOU CANNOT FIND *it in nature or at your local grocery store, it was born by a pre-existing notion of things fresh, sweet, unique, and lush — all attributes that can make an ordinary wedding extraordinary by letting your dreams become a reality.*

we learn that fanciful childhood ideas must be tempered. We no longer expect anything to be "perfect" — except when it comes to our wedding day!

This is the one day when these dreamlike visions are still allowed to transform themselves into reality — and even the most down-to-earth woman often finds herself longing to feel like that perfect princess. Weddings are the only times that people allow themselves to be something from a fairy tale; the only time that people want to go (and, in fact, give themselves permission to go) where they've never been before. It doesn't have to be an over-the-top or elaborate vision — it could be anything. Dreams and fantasies vary from person to person as much as style of expression varies from artist to artist. No vision of a wedding is "wrong" or "too much" — unless it's too much for you.

The first event I ever designed was in 1982 — the wedding of Dr. Betsy Levy at the Rainbow Room in Rockefeller Plaza. I have to laugh when I realize how naïve I was at the time — how I nodded vigorously when she described her vision of the chuppah. I went straight back to my tiny office and grabbed a dictionary — I had no idea what a chuppah was, much less how to design one! Since then I've produced thousands of events, from

a romantic two-person anniversary surprise dinner aboard a private yacht to a six-hundred-guest A-list celebrity wedding in midtown Manhattan. Each has a special place in my heart because each one was an extraordinarily personal mix of imagination and artistry between my client and me.

There is an amazing amount of trust put into my hands when it comes to an event like a wedding, and I always feel blessed that people place such confidence in me for an extremely personal and important moment in their lives. But I don't do it alone — the visions are collaborations among the bride, the groom, usually their parents, and me. The execution is a carefully orchestrated dance between my preparatory staff and setup crew. Without them, I couldn't create the elaborate and ornate visions you'll see in this book.

Depending on the event, I usually meet with clients three to six months before the date to start talking about ideas. We talk about everything, and at the initial meeting I usually end up asking more questions than I answer. After all, it's not about me and *my* favorite flower — it's about them and their visions of their day. My job is to

interpret their preferences, tastes, and, yes, their fantasies — and make them a reality. I ask them about colors,

feelings, and what they would want in their ideal wedding. Sometimes they only have a single adjective or mood,

and interpreting this through their eyes is the key to creating their vision. Of course, other factors are important, including budget, location, and time of year. All the elements are brought together in my office, where my next steps are to translate them into what the couple wants.

The number of times I meet with clients between our initial consultation and the actual day of the wedding depends on the couple's needs and on how quickly we decide on a final design plan. For some it takes only two meetings, but for others a bit more searching is required. The most important thing is that we are conceptually and stylistically on the same page. At the presentation meeting, I actually put together one of the reception tables — complete with full centerpiece, place settings, linens, and glassware — in order to let the couple see for themselves what their guests will experience. At this point we make any adjustments they feel are necessary, or (as is sometimes the case) readjust our visions and start with another approach. In the end, I meet with clients until they are comfortable that I am interpreting and translating their personal vision correctly.

I've orchestrated events in all sorts of environments, from the tropical sands of Turks and Caicos, to the gilded architecture of the Plaza Hotel, to the minimal decor of a modern loft apartment in Manhattan. But whatever the location, when you're working with a designer, it's important both to communicate what you want and to not micromanage the designer's style. After all, you've presumably seen enough samples of their work and spoken to enough references to know that you like their technique, so at a certain point, you should feel comfortable enough to let go and enjoy yourself.

TRUSTING YOUR DESIGNER CAN MEAN THE DIFFERENCE BETWEEN a stress-free event and a long-term headache. You should be communicative and comfortable with your designer to the point where you are able — during the big day — to let go of the reins and simply enjoy the vision you've created together.

The most common request I get is not for a specific color, flower, theme, or style — it's to make "something that's never been seen before." People come to me looking for something that's different and unique; something more than reality; something that's possibly never even been *conceived of* before. To me, it's not just about the flowers — it's about the stimulation of the senses through light, texture, patterns, and color. This is what is so exciting about what I do — every day I'm challenged to think in new ways and experiment with ideas and concepts. And that to me is the true definition of fantasy.

Inspirations come from many places, and I find that most of the time I get my most creative ideas simply by paying attention to the world around me. One place I constantly look to is nature. It seems so simple — nature is what's around you all the time, and most of us never take a second glance. But if you stop and take a moment to look a bit closer, you'll notice that even in the simplest things you can find amazing ideas.

I love taking an element of nature — a single petal, a branch of leaves, the colors of a dragonfly wing, or even just the notion of repeated shape — and mimicking it in as many ways as possible. I work with elements of nature every day — flowers, leaves, wood, petals, vines. Nature is beautiful in its structure and design, from the imposing strength of the tallest evergreen to the smallest and most delicate vein running through a single petal. If I'm in the city, I wander the flower markets and see something new every time. Whether it's a rose of a particular hue or an orchid that I've never seen before, I love the freshness and unassumingly perfect beauty of flowers and the emotions that they evoke. I am constantly surprised and inspired by the beauty of the natural world,

FROM THE LARGEST FLORAL SCULPTURES
SUSPENDED FROM THE CEILING TO THE
*smallest votives at each place setting, attention to
detail is paramount. The more intimate touches
are essential to making guests feel welcome and
comfortable, even in the most elaborate settings.*

which is the reason I adore working with its elements. It is this simplicity, repeated on many layers, that often yields the most dramatic results and impacts the senses in profound ways.

It's an interesting juxtaposition, since I am perhaps best known for my larger-than-life floral sculptures — quite a contrast to the small things that I am influenced by. But it's in taking these small elements and changing them — reshaping them into larger, more dramatic statements — that the energy and excitement emerge.

I define my creations as sculptures — sculptures with flowers. And while it takes an incredible amount of patience and is meticulous work, the results are astounding. My constructions transform flowers in a variety of interesting ways — by removing hundreds of rose petals and gluing them one by one onto a place mat; or threading thousands of miniature orchids into ten-foot strands to frame windows or doorways; or even pinning, by the thousands, individual leaves onto the body of a lion sculpture to introduce the perfect and unique centerpiece for a cocktail hour. Whether it's an oversized, petal-covered lantern hanging from the ceiling of a huge tent or a small floating rose in a glass bowl, each is inspired by the petals it is sculpted from, which are merely reinterpreted and reshaped into vastly different forms. Admittedly, I've asked my crew to do (and often joined them in doing) some pretty bizarre and outrageous things — but the end result is always worth it.

One aspect of my life that I consistently draw upon for motivation is my Latin heritage. Being born in Panama, I grew up surrounded by vibrant colors and lush foliage. As a result, I love working with colors and contrasts as much as possible. Colors have a complex life of their own and can speak in so many different ways, depending on the context in which they are used and how they are interpreted. And I'm not just referring to flowers here — lighting, architecture, fabrics, and even glassware can bring in color statements that can change the entire mood of the surroundings. Experimenting with color is an adventure on so many levels!

I'm an open-minded designer and love hearing new ideas or visions from clients. (One exception comes to mind, however. I once had a client who requested all-black flower arrangements for her wedding. While that wasn't the only reason I declined their event, it certainly was a concept I'd never heard of before.) The most unusual request I've ever had was to design an event that, according to the invitees, wasn't even happening. It was a surprise destination wedding in St. Martin. The couple had been dating for a long time, and wanted to invite family and friends down for a weekend party in the Caribbean. They did not tell their guests, however, that we were planning a surprise wedding, so all the arrangements were made on the sly.

Obviously, setting up some events takes longer than others, with the majority of long-term setups involving the assembly of large tents. Usually we have one or even two weeks to do major setups or build necessary constructions. There are some locations, however, that won't allow you on the premises until a certain hour, and this has certainly pushed my crew to their limits. The shortest setup time I've ever had was only three hours, and we had to transform a room into a completely new setting. Of course the more elements you have and the shorter the time, the larger the setup crew needs to be — so I hired a small army for that event, and the controlled chaos and adrenaline rush of the situation still makes my heart beat fast when I think about it.

While I've never dropped a wedding cake (wisely, I'm not responsible for them), I've had my fair share of near disasters over the years. The most stressful was probably a wedding event in New York, scheduled for a balmy Saturday in August 2003 (see chapter 3). Two days prior to the wedding, at approximately 4:15 p.m., the power went out in portions of the United States — including all of Manhattan . . . and my refrigeration units. Surprisingly, and much to my relief, most of the flowers survived in good shape, and we only lost about 25 per-cent of the blooms. But the challenge didn't stop, since most of my crew was unable to make it into the city for setup. That was a long weekend, I have to admit. But in the end (and after pulling an all-night vigil), the event worked out beautifully. After all, it's a wedding — not something that's easily postponed. And part of my job is to perform under pressure . . . you just hope that the pressure eases up on the next one!

It's hard to describe yourself through others' eyes, but most of my clients say that I'm a comfort to them and that I make the experience fun. After all, my business depends on pleasing the clients that hire me — as it does in any service industry. And when they hire me to handle something as important as a wedding day, I feel it's an

honor to be trusted with such a precious moment in someone's life. At the same time, however, I do want them to have a good time! So my goal for every event is not only to make them feel comfortable enough to trust me with their event, but also to give them a chance to truly experience an amazing and unforgettable time in their lives without worrying if the centerpieces will arrive on time.

The most nerve-racking moment for me is when the guests arrive and see my work for the very first time. This is my moment of truth. The initial reactions are the most honest, and I often find myself standing in the shadows next to the entrance with butterflies in my stomach, anticipating the first guests' entrance. My reward is encapsulated in those precious moments; in those first gasps or comments muttered as they enter the world I created. Nothing is more rewarding to me than witnessing those seconds when I know that I've introduced them to something that they've never seen before — and will probably never see again.

CREATING SOMETHING THAT'S NEVER EXISTED BEFORE — THIS IS NOT ONLY *the dream of every artist, but also the essence of transforming a fantasy into reality. Reaching out and stretching the imagination for something new is challenging, but when everything comes together into one vision, nothing is more rewarding.*

The weddings in this book are some of the most lavish and rich creations I've ever put together. Keep in mind that each is as much a personal statement about the couple as it is about my style and design concepts. In the final chapter, I'll introduce you to my Signature collection — a line of floral sculptures and elements that I hope will inspire you to look further and help you reach your own floral stylistic vision. You'll probably recognize some of the elements in Signature in the weddings featured in this book. This way, you can see them in context, as well as standing on their own.

To start planning your own fantasy wedding, start with what you know best — your own taste. Think of something that fits you and your personality. What are you most comfortable with? Do you love the look of a French château? Or is a modern art gallery more your taste? Do you love vibrant and bright colors, or do you lean towards more subdued or subtle tones? After all, even if this is the most precious day you've planned for in your life so far, you still want to be comfortable with the final vision. Then, once you figure out the basics, take them and make your vision larger than life! Dream about it, and push it just one or two steps further. After all, fantasy is about being a little bit out there, and reaching for something you wouldn't otherwise think possible . . . so go for it!

As you read this book, I only have one piece of advice: Allow yourself to dream. I define fantasy as something that appears to be unreachable — but in an inspiring and challenging way. It's something to strive for — a goal, a vision. Sometimes creating the reality will be successful, and sometimes not. But reaching for it is what fantasy is all about.

CHAPTER ONE

Glorious Glasshouse Fantasy

MY INSPIRATIONS FOR WEDDING DESIGNS SPRING FROM A SURPRISING VARIETY OF SOURCES. I'VE NEVER BELIEVED IN THE TRADITIONAL path, so rarely do I look for a traditional source of inspiration. And while flowers are usually the primary focus of my clients, I've found that the environment itself often deserves as much (or more) attention as the floral decor.

For their summer wedding in the Hamptons, one young couple knew what they wanted and had very specific requests. They wanted to have the wedding and reception in their large backyard, but did not want a typical tent setup.

For the reception I had to hunt a bit for ideas for our temporary structure. I came up with a particularly romantic architectural structure called the glasshouse. These original mid-nineteenth-century conservatories were forged from iron and glass, creating a gorgeous filigree of metalwork that covered lush indoor gardens. Filled with tropical plants, statues, artwork, and fountains, these glasshouses were designed for the sole purpose of entertainment and socializing — a perfect match for our wedding utopia!

During the nineteenth century, industrialization resulted in a huge influx of people to major cities, and the city dwellers longed for a return to nature. The exquisite iron-and-glass glasshouse was a living terrarium, created to display striking plants from faraway lands under a larger-than-life glass "jar." These grand creations quickly became a symbol of higher-class beauty and wealth and were built to promote a social utopia. Guests would spend hours mingling, enjoying banquets and even concerts among the many fountains and flora enclosed under the ornate glass domes.

For our couple's wedding and reception, I could not bring in iron and glass — it would have been prohibitively expensive, not to mention dangerous if any of the glass broke. So we reinterpreted the traditional style with modern materials, yet still maintained the nod to the nineteenth-century ideals of shape and composition. We created a transparent glasslike effect in contrast to the colored glass we constructed for the ceremony. I used clear Plexiglas and semi-opaque fabrics to mimic translucent glass panes along the walls and lofty, domed ceiling. Since the original glasshouses flaunted their filigree ironwork, we kept the structural lines visible and bright from floor to ceiling, celebrating the elements of the construction itself.

LOOSE CLUSTERS OF FLOWERS HIGH-
LIGHTED IN THE CENTERPIECES (ABOVE)
*reflect the glasshouse ideal of displaying flora
naturally and allow each bloom to have its own
space. Keeping the colors simple and clean avoids
a cluttered feel and instead creates a cohesive,
organic statement.*

THE SEMIOPAQUE FABRIC WALLS OF
THE GLASSHOUSE-INSPIRED TENT WERE
*softly lit from behind (opposite and overleaf).
It was almost as if soft sunlight were streaming
through the panes, even though this was an
evening celebration.*

One of the most important aspects of the original glasshouse design was lighting. As it was meant to be flooded with daylight, the ideal construction would be infused with uniform brightness, with no dark shadows or corners to be found. Since our reception was held in the evening, we didn't have the sun to help us out, and the illumination became a major challenge. But brilliant lighting designer Bentley Meeher surpassed my expectations, and masterfully backlit the entire structure to achieve the dazzling environment I wanted.

The airy feeling continued through the rest of the decor. Several important design elements were incorporated into the walls, including recessed niches to display open floral arrangements atop four-foot pedestals. To add to the luminous surroundings, the pedestals were lit from the inside, so the flowers appeared to float on light itself. To contrast with these recessed arrangements, we alternated displays of different floral vines that seemed to grow on the walls themselves. True to our glasshouse inspiration, each panel high-lighted a different kind of bloom, including hydrangea bunches, hanging hand-sewn rose-petal wisterias, and

GLASS PLACE SETTINGS (OPPOSITE)
NOT ONLY EXTENDED THE GLASSHOUSE
*inspiration, but also subtly reflected the light
streaming in from the tent sides. The green
wineglasses added a spark of color and complemented the soft-hued tablecloth perfectly.*

THE ARCHITECTURAL LINES OF THE
TENT ADDED A NATURALLY AUTHENTIC
*touch to the glasshouse design idea. We enhanced
the premise by adding recessed areas to display
floral arrangements (right) and backlit "windows."*

Nepenthes. Each display consisted of a digital printed image of flowers on a scrim and adorned with real flowers, again lit from behind. Several hundred more wisteria creations swung gently from the rafters over the dance floor.

We used only three colors in the room: celadon, white, and green. Using cool, calm colors during the hot summer months lends a breath of fresh air to events and lightens up the atmosphere. In addition, when I use such a wide variety of loose flowers in a large space, I find it's best to stick to simple and neat colors. Otherwise, structure and continuity can get lost in the clash of too many competing hues.

We created two alternating centerpieces for the tables — some tall enough to stand above the guests and some shorter to bring the gaze down to a more intimate level. The taller creations were high and open, incorporating Bells of Ireland, roses, and oversized green-and-white calla lilies reaching out of a tall, clear glass flute. Inside the body of the flute, we hung a single hand-sewn wisteria, created by threading individual rose petals on wire. The orchid-covered boxes of the low centerpieces held an organic display of white roses, sweet peas, Bells of Ireland, and lisianthus.

The tables were draped in green raw silk with soft linen overlays embroidered with fern and ribbon patterns. Clear table settings echoed the uncluttered lines and glass details, but I also added unexpected green wineglasses for a flash of color. Square pillar candles on frosted saucers added a romantic touch, and juxtaposed nicely with the round shape of the tables. Sisal carpeting and bamboo ballroom chairs completed the setting and kept the experience natural, elegant, and refined.

For the wedding ceremony, we re-created a synagogue on the grounds, complete with "stained-glass" windows — also located within a tent! Creating the tent structures was the most challenging aspect of the event: how to create another glasslike effect — without using glass. So I used Plexiglas and printed semiopaque fabrics to mimic the stained glass along the walls and tiles behind the altar. Motivation originated from a synagogue's arched pillars and loftlike ceiling, so we duplicated the idea for our environment.

For the stained-glass windows, we re-created the famous windows that were designed by Marc Chagall for the synagogue of the Hadassah University Hospital in Israel. Michael Speir printed the artwork onto fabric scrims, which were then framed and backlit to conjure up the glow of evening sunlight streaming through the panes. Populated by images of flora, fauna, fish, and flowers, the gem-colored windows perfectly complemented the serene atmosphere. They were topped by domed "windows" of stained glass patterned after the Star of David. For the altar, we re-created on scrims the traditional symbols of the dove, the tree of life, the menorah, and the Ten Commandments. Four-foot Moroccan lanterns were suspended from the ceiling, adding to the Moorish environment, and filling the space in the lofty ceiling. The only floral touches were explosions of blue delphiniums located behind the altar.

"STAINED-GLASS" WINDOW AND ARCH DESIGNS (ABOVE) WERE MADE OF FABRIC *and lit from behind, which allowed the vibrant colors to glow.*

A SYNAGOGUE-INSPIRED TENT ALMOST LOOKS LIKE THE REAL THING (OPPOSITE). *Since tradition was so important to the bride and groom, we incorporated many religious symbols into the designs around the room.*

The synagogue environment was important to this couple, as well as reverence to upholding family traditions. The groom's grandmothers' chuppah was carried during the ceremony by the bride's brothers. Using personal and handmade touches for any small element of the wedding helps to bring the guests into the lives of the bride and groom, making the event even more meaningful for everyone in attendance.

This event was one of my favorites, not because it was easy (quite the contrary), but simply because everything worked together into a unified environment. Even though we didn't use one pane of glass or one iron rod, I feel as though we captured the ideals of the synagogue and the ethereal architecture and social environment of the glasshouse. I was lucky in this particular situation, as I had nearly two weeks to build the tents, as well as the assistance of a genius lighting designer. Rarely do I have the privilege of this amount of time to create a utopian milieu — and we used every moment of it! It goes to show that inspiration can come from any place, past or present.

Hamptons Countryside Fantasy

WHEN I TRAVEL AROUND THE WORLD GIVING LECTURES AND SEMINARS, I INEVITABLY MEET NUMEROUS PEOPLE WITH DISTINCTIVE

personalities. I remember meeting one woman who approached me excitedly after a presentation on floral sculpturing, and told

me that she'd *love* to have me design her daughter's wedding. I, of course, replied that I would be happy to work with her, and

asked if the happy couple had settled on a date. To this she responded, "Oh, she's not engaged yet . . . but as soon as she is, I'm

going to give you a call!" Less than two months later, my phone rang — her daughter was engaged, and we were on for a fantasy

wedding in the Hamptons!

The gorgeous Watermill property was set on the highest point in the Hamptons, overlooking the green rolling hills of the

countryside. This historic community and surrounding landscape was the perfect place for a tent wedding and the ideal backdrop

for the country-inspired decor. The ceremony adornment consisted of a single bold statement under a transparent tent: a lush

floral chuppah. The tent allowed an unobstructed view of the surrounding land and kept nature close at hand. The chuppah itself

was an organic construction of white birch tree trunks laced with a myriad of cream and pale-colored flowers. I wanted to create the illusion that the structure was built out of the rambling rose, hydrangea, and wisteria clusters. This lush creation was an elegant contrast to the clean, clear lines of the tent around it. After all, if you want a particular element to stand out in any design, the best way to do it is to contrast it with its surroundings.

The reception for the 180 guests was held in another tent nearby, and echoed the bride and groom's desire to give the event an intimate, comfortable feeling. The gathered fabric of

the draped roof brought the gaze upwards towards several oversized hanging baskets suspended from the ceiling. Instead of using traditional rattan or wood for the bases, I sculpted the baskets with woven leaves and berries, echoing the shape of handmade rustic creations. Bursting from each and cascading over the edges were hundreds of the same rose, hydrangea, and wisteria blooms that were in the chuppah, but this time in bright earthy tones of orange, burgundy, red, and purple. Overflowing these baskets were hand-sewn orchid details, which brought the eye down towards the tall centerpieces. The colors were strong in this setting. It's important to remember when working with bright, bold colors to keep a balance by setting them on a subtle background. This way, you complement your color statements and do not compete with them.

We decided to use long tables for the guests. On each table stood two tall centerpieces, sculpted with the same leaves as the baskets overhead. Each stood about five feet tall, constructed with foam core. The base, layered with leaves, was pinched at the midline with bright roses. From there, the sculptural designs exploded upwards into a large floral arrangement created with hundreds of roses, hydrangea, and orchids. Draping from the sides were several hand-sewn rose-petal wisteria with berry detailing. The time it took to create each of the hanging baskets and large centerpieces was remarkable, since each leaf, flower, and berry had to be individually woven, pinned, or glued to the inner framework. The smaller centerpieces repeated the same flowers, and we added several bowls of floating roses to bring the details to the most intimate levels of the dinner. The tablecloths continued the organic country feel — green velvet-embossed chiffon overlays graced raw-silk taupe underlays. Each guest was greeted at their place setting with a cluster of budding flowers tucked into the carefully folded napkins.

At the bar, I introduced a sculpture that echoed the shapes of the taller centerpieces but also brought in the same basket idea used in the hanging arrangements. Built with an open latticework of dark twigs, I attached clusters of hydrangea, roses, and berries to give it a lush feel — as if it were straight from the outdoors. While this is a rather large statement in a relatively small area, the open latticework at the base balanced it nicely.

Into every perfect event, however, a little rain must fall, and the New England mid-September weather gave us a misty, gray day. At first, we were prepared to be disappointed. But as it turned out, it lent a surreal, dreamlike quality that actually emphasized the bright colors of the floral creations and enhanced the fantasy of the setting.

The dance floor was another central design statement, and one that I'm particularly proud of. Motivated by the inlaid marble patterns found in estates in the area, we designed our own floor pattern and printed it out in large tiles. Pieced together, the floor was a centerpiece for the entire room. It was a beautiful complement to the other elements around the room, and brought attention and drama to the center of the room without interrupting the open dance space or the views.

As with any situation, there are certain clients one hopes to never encounter again, and there are others who are wonderful to work with. This event fell into the latter category — dream clients that I yearn for. From the initial meeting with the bride and groom to the final wedding day, our styles and personalities connected seamlessly, and to this day, we still get together for lunch whenever our schedules allow. Every event is special for me. But when a client and I communicate so well, as we did in this case, an unparalled element of trust is placed in my hands. These moments are especially close to my heart, and I feel almost as though I am designing a party for myself or a family member. After all, when you're a key player in the most important day in a couple's life, you want to make it a day that no one will ever forget.

CHAPTER THREE

Modern Metropolitan Fantasy

THERE ARE TIMES WHEN COUPLES COME TO ME AND SAY, "DO WHATEVER YOU WANT!," AND THAT IS SO EXCITING! THERE ARE rare instances when, as an artist, I thrive on the creative freedom that this allows me. But this independence is tempered by the pressure to live up to the reputation that precedes me. While the brides- and grooms-to-be give me license to do whatever *I* want, the reality is that I am given the responsibility of finding a style that suits the client best. Combining my own creative juices with the clients' styles can sometimes get tricky, but fortunately, I've become quite adept at finding a balance between my own style and the couple's vision.

To start this sometimes daunting process, I begin by asking questions about a couple's life — and not just about their design preferences. By finding out about other elements of their lives, I discover important clues that they may think are irrelevant. I ask them about favorite places they vacationed or visited, artists they are particularly fond of, or colors, ideas, or fashion styles they are inspired by.

THE BRIGHT ORANGE HIGHLIGHTS IN THE
COLOR SCHEME INSPIRED ME TO DESIGN MY
*own tropical bloom (left). At each place setting,
the guests had their own version of my Balinese-
inspired flower, made with Leucospermum blooms,
feathers, and orchids.*

THE HUES ARE CLEAN AND CONTEMPORARY,
BUT HIGHLIGHTING WITH A FEW POPS
*of color and texture — like the bright orange
kumquats (opposite) — adds depth and dimension
to the design elements. Don't be afraid to experiment with the unexpected and exotic.*

In this case, a very "New York" affair was held in a huge white studio overlooking the Hudson River. As the couple loved Balinese culture and style, we decided to go with a colorful yet contemporary feel. The room was a blank white canvas with two walls of windows overlooking the stunning cityscape, and was primarily used as a set for films and for high-fashion photo shoots. It was the perfect opportunity to create our own environment from scratch. That's one of the best things about empty spaces — they allow you to expand in stylistic directions often unsupported by predecorated locales or distinctive architectural styles.

For the ceremony, the two hundred guests were seated on diagonally placed benches and stools flanking the aisle. The walls were covered in white raw-silk fabric. This allowed a soft yet structured look, while still maintaining a separation between the ceremonial space and the reception area. Trees were built from birch branches, green vines, and floral clusters created from white Dendrobium orchids. We only used a single type of flower for the entire ceremony, which when paired with the bold fabrics, streamlined everything beautifully, and kept the overall feeling polished and formal, not stiff or overly austere.

TAKE INSPIRATION FROM YOUR LOCATION
WHEN LOOKING FOR IDEAS. THE STRAIGHT
*architectural lines of the loft's open space (previous
spread) are echoed in the lines of the decor, blending
perfectly into a cohesive idea that encompasses the
whole room.*

The reception dinner decor was detailed with Balinese touches. Inspired by the room itself, uninterrupted lines and neat corners dictated the symmetrical, modern designs. What guests noticed first were the eight-foot draped structures held aloft over the long rectangular tables. The two-tiered shapes were built using metal frames, with tiny green orchids draped gracefully above the guests' heads. Tipped with Japanese lanterns (Physalis *alkekengi*), their contrasting hues and textures created a color scheme in sync with the architecturally inspired shape and filled the open space of the studio perfectly.

Gracing the length of the tables, elongated box-shaped centerpieces featured kumquats, orange petals, and orchids. These long, low shapes exaggerated the length of the table by continuing the symmetry at a much more intimate level. For each place setting we also created our own "flower" — round creations using Leucospermum blooms, small feathers, and orchids. Each setting also featured a fan silk-screened with a peacock feather that served as the place card as well as the menu. In a similar twist, guests were assigned seats at tables designated by names of various sentiments: Peace, Hope, Happiness, Love, Health, and Harmony, to name a few. A few square votives finished the romantic feel and added a touch of cozy lighting.

The long dining tables and chairs were covered with striped green cloth which emphasized the architectural lines and color palette. On the back of each seat we hung fans — inspired not only by the Balinese idea but also by the oppressive heat of the summer month. Fans alternated between oversized green leaf creations and feather clusters. They were the perfect organic complement to the otherwise contemporary surroundings, rounding out the warm sentiments of the Balinese detailing.

WE PULLED TOGETHER THIS ENTIRE EVENT DURING A MAJOR BLACKOUT — *no one in the city had electricity! Fortunately, using hardy blooms helped prevent a disaster, and we didn't lose much to the August heat.*

DURING DINNER, THE ORIGINAL CEREMONY AREA WAS MAGICALLY *converted to a hot nightclub dance floor (below left). Since the space was white, we were able to completely transform the room with brilliant, sharply colored lighting effects.*

But while the design fit seamlessly with the surrounding line and structure, we weren't as lucky with the preparation and setup. We are always ready to have some unexpected problems, but this time we had to deal with a natural disaster beyond our

MUTED GOLD-RIMMED PLACE SETTINGS (ABOVE) *added a subtle sheen to the event, and organic leaves on each napkin kept the feeling close to nature. Use your imagination — paying attention to details like this can really add a distinctive mark to your event.*

control. This particular occasion was preceded by the massive blackout of 2003! Thirty-six hours before the event, most of the northeastern United States lost power. As a result, the refrigeration for the premade arrangements shut off in the midst of the sweltering August heat. When the power was finally restored and I was able to access the arrangements in our refrigeration rooms, I was pleasantly surprised (and very relieved) to see that only about 25 percent of the blooms had wilted during the

THIS IS A PERFECT COMBINATION OF THE *organic inspiration of Bali and the urban sophistication of Manhattan. Small twists on the expected kept the decor interesting and exciting. In this case, silk screen–printed fans on each place setting (opposite) served as unique seating cards.*

90-degree day. While I lucked out with the hardy blooms, the problems didn't stop there. Usually setup involves a small army of men and women descending upon the location to build the structures. But because public transportation was shut down for so long, we worked with only a skeleton crew.

THE WHITE-HUED CEREMONY
OFFERS SERENE RESPITE FROM
*the bustling city outside. The decor
is composed but not severe, and
the soft fabrics and angled seating
combined with the organic trees
is pure — and not stuffy. Even the
walls are fabric-covered panels.
We weren't permitted to touch the
existing walls, so we built our own.*

In addition, the space agreement dictated that we were not allowed to touch the walls or ceiling with any fixtures or hanging elements. Each silk wall and tall, overhanging centerpiece had to be completely independent and unattached to the ceiling or walls of the room. I equate it with creating a set for the theater: everything looks permanent and real but is actually meant to be taken down and carted away after the show ends. By the grace of good fortune, things worked out well despite the national state of emergency, but I'll be glad if I never have to climb up that many flights of stairs to a loft space again.

After dinner, guests were invited back to the ceremony area, which had been transformed into a hot dance club. Blue lights and club music pulsed for hours, and the night's sparkling skyline rounded out the evening. The entire event was a perfect example of how to use surrounding space and architecture to your advantage. Inspired by the modern lines of the white studio around us, we paired clean shapes with unique flowers and whimsical touches, creating the perfect midcity fantasy for a contemporary celebration.

THIS BRIGHT PROFUSION OF PETALS AND COLORS (above) was my original concept for this couple's reception. It was distinctly different from the final Balinese fantasy we eventually created and is a perfect example of how visions change as I work with the client.

THE LESS ARCHITECTURAL DESIGNS INCLUDED A FUN "petal cup" (opposite), made with individual rose petals and topped with a bright cluster of berries. This and the two perfect blooms tucked into the napkins offered guests a wonderful, intimate feeling.

CHAPTER FOUR

Tropical Latin Fantasy

REHEARSAL DINNER: A CELEBRATION OF ROSES

FREQUENTLY, FAMILY MEMBERS, COMING FROM ALL PARTS OF THE GLOBE, HAVE TO TRAVEL GREAT DISTANCES to attend a wedding. Weddings have become multiday affairs in order to accommodate and entertain guests who could be staying up to a week for the celebration. In addition to the reception, more and more guests are attending the traditional rehearsal dinner, which is therefore becoming a far more formalized event, as we'll see here.

One of the main reasons this particular couple came to me for their event was because of my Panamanian heritage, which aligned closely with the bride's family roots. They knew I'd incorporate flair, and they wanted something that had never been done before for both the rehearsal dinner and wedding reception. In this case, the bride's large extended family flew in from South America for a traditional Latin celebration that lasted for almost a week.

At our first meeting, the twenty-three-year-old bride knew she wanted roses — and lots of them. When a young bride comes to see me, often she wants something different and more exciting than the expected traditional decor. The challenge is to take her idea and transform it into something inspired without losing the essence of her fantasy vision. Luckily enough, this bride was very close to her mother, and the three of us worked together in perfect harmony (a rare treat, let me tell you!). Their vivacious spirit allowed me to be more imaginative and to design more whimsical elements than usual. They wanted to be surprised — along with their guests — at a larger-than-life tropical homage to their culture.

The rehearsal dinner was held at the Museum of Natural History in New York City. The open space and the couple's energetic personalities fused perfectly into this revelation of artistic romance. When I'm planning designs, my inspiration can come from many sources, but sometimes the decisive motivation comes from a deceptively simple place. In this case, we knew we wanted vibrant-colored roses, but we also wanted a bit of enchantment and surprise! I decided to mix things up a little. But this didn't mean thinking bigger . . . it meant thinking *smaller*. Instead of taking an entire rose as the element of design, I focused on the simplest element of the bloom: the petal. The entire event space was filled with brilliant pink and red rose petals, and they were worked into every different design element. But it's too predictable to sprinkle petals randomly on dinner tables; instead I strewed them all over the room in more dynamic ways.

ROSE PETALS WERE EVERYWHERE, FROM THE PLACE MATS (ABOVE) TO the individual petals tucked into each napkin. Every petal was inspected before the event and any with browning edges were replaced before the guests arrived.

ROSE PETALS ACCENTED THE ROOM AT EVERY LEVEL (PREVIOUS SPREAD), FROM the suspended rose drapes to the tiniest details on the place mats. We used thousands of roses for this room, nearly emptying the flower market suppliers.

To add depth and dimension, layering became a central design feature. I created layers of petals on both a large and small scale within the event space. While seated at the tables, guests were encircled by petals: overhead, under the place settings, and delicately tucked into their napkins. Even the place mats were built from linen fabric templates onto which were affixed layers of individual petals of different hues. The single-petal theme was reflected in the hand-folded napkins. This multilevel application of design technique makes any facet more interesting and enjoyable. Each table also had six square glass bowls in which we floated roses surrounded by petals in a radiating pattern. This presented the illusion of a single huge, graceful rose in each bowl.

The glassware was chosen to complement the artistic and energetic feel of the design. Since we didn't want the glasses and plates to compete with or hide the roses, we used clear, unadorned pieces, allowing the guests to see through their plates to the petal place mats beneath. This kept the look contemporary and clean and ensured that no detail at the table would be missed. The glass added shine and sparkle, reflecting the high-energy lights and colors of the event.

Whether found in the roses or napkins or place mats, the color palette included variations on vibrant reds and hot pinks, meant to embrace the Latin American background of the couple and their families. Even the round banquette seating and long benches were draped in the hot tropical colors of the day. Special blush-pink lights streamed through the hanging petal shades, adding a glimmer to the room as guests mingled. From the romance of a single candle flame to the excitement of bold, flashing lights in a large dance hall, illumination can alter the entire mood and energy of your event.

The roses themselves are another obvious and important tool for these designs. While most people think of flowers as short-lived and delicate objects, I work with particularly hardy blooms, since the preparation for complex sculptural pieces often starts ten days in advance of the event. Flowers must be treated well by cleaning them properly upon their delivery, changing their water daily, and keeping them in a cool room so they will look as fresh and healthy on day ten as they did the day they were cut. Since I was working in such large quantities here, careful treatment of the thousands of roses was no small task. As you can see, the real vision is in the details. Thousands

of hours were spent separating the millions of individual petals and then meticulously threading, gluing, pinning, or hanging them one at a time to create the elements in the environment. With all the manhandling that the petals went through, it was important to treat them with care from the moment they arrived in my studio.

Since both the bride and groom are involved with the art world, I was a bit more adventurous than usual with the sculptural elements around the room. Their youth, energy, and vivacious personalities inspired me to perhaps take these a bit further than I would for an older couple or a more reserved event. But it certainly worked here, and the couple was overwhelmed by the rose fantasy. Looking at the overall room, they saw petals descending from the ceiling, wrapping poles at midlevel, adorning the floral sculptures, and coating place mats at tables that held bowls of floating roses.

Building fantasies such as this takes more than just flowers and imagination — and since no detail is overlooked — only the best quality will do. For everything to come together requires endless patience, hours of time, and tireless crews of specialists, all working towards the same vision of one perfect fantasy atmosphere.

The unbelievably talented salsa band kept guests dancing until the wee hours. But this was just a warm-up for the reception the next day, held at the Cipriani Ballroom. The tropical inspiration continued there, but with a much different interpretation . . . and I'm still trying to figure out how the couple and their family had the energy to keep partying all weekend!

BAMBOO IS A LIVELY AND SURPRISINGLY
ARCHITECTURAL MEDIUM TO WORK WITH
*(left and opposite). While it's beautifully organic,
it still maintains a structured feel. I loved the
contrast between the clean bamboo lines and the
softer shapes of the orchids.*

THE TROPICAL SUNSET PRINTED ON
THE ELEVEN-PANEL SCREEN (OVERLEAF)
*separated the cocktail area from the reception
dinner, providing a gorgeous delineation between
spaces. The architecture of the Cipriani Ballroom
was a surprising complement to the natural shapes.*

THE RECEPTION:
A FABULOUS FIESTA

As the guests entered the impressive Italian renaissance architecture of Cipriani 42nd Street, they were immediately swept away into a lush, sultry rain forest. What I love most about what I do is the ability to generate environments that would never exist in certain places — and are only possible in dreams.

Over four hundred guests were served cocktails in front of ten printed scrims depicting a glorious tropical sunset. The panels were primarily intended to conceal the main dining room until dinner was ready. However, lit from behind, the glowing silk-screened scrims also served to set the tropical rain forest experience for the guests, many of whom flew in from Brazil for the weekend's festivities. The cocktail tables, on either side of the grand foyer, held bamboo-stem sculptures, accented with oversized orchids and tied together with fringed raffia to complete the lush atmosphere. Since the stunning architecture and intricate designs of the decor were so luxuriant, we used simple white plates to complement them. With the environment established, guests were invited to enjoy tropical drinks and zesty hors d'oeuvres that completed the mood.

As dinner was announced, the scrims parted to reveal the incredible, larger-than-life Amazonian rain forest we had built in the main dining area. As if you were entering the wilds of the forest itself, everything was made to seem as if it were teeming with tropical flora and fauna on a grand scale. If at first we thought the 1921 architecture would seem incongruous, the sixty-five-foot ceilings actually added to the grand canopy feel and supported our idea of playing with scale.

To keep up the sultry fantasy, I used an abundance of flowers to craft objects that weren't technically possible. We played with colors and created sculptural interpretations of real objects. Oversized pineapples, sculpted with hundreds of miniature pink roses, elephant's ears, and pink Dendrobium orchids, accented the buffet tables. Standing watch over the seat assignment cards was a sacred cow, meticulously covered from head to toe with hand-folded lemon leaves and orchids. As you can see, we really played up the whimsical elements of the event — and the bride and groom were up for the challenge of keeping things fun and light. Even for such a formal event as a wedding, no one should be afraid to have some fun — that's what a party is all about. Not only do fanciful or unusual ornamental elements liven up the atmosphere, but they can be great conversation starters as well.

When planning the colors for a sultry party of any size, it's far too predictable to use standard red. So we kicked things up with hot pinks and oranges, which hearkened back to the pinks at the rehearsal dinner and which were also included in the bride's bouquet.

OVERSIZED FLORAL "PINEAPPLES" (ABOVE), BUILT WITH MINIATURE FLOWERS AND *leaves sprouting from the top. in various colors added to the tropical aura in the room.*

THE COLORS WE USED FOR ALL OF THE DECOR STAYED TRUE TO THE TROPICAL *influence, and we stuck to our hues regardless of the subject matter. And somehow, pink pineapples (opposite) fit right in.*

The tablecloths were combinations of warm colors: pinks with a striped burgundy linen, and orange with scarlet overlays. Centerpieces needed to match the grand scale of the event and therefore were built to tower eight feet over the tabletops. Inside the centerpieces, underneath the miniature roses and hand-set leaves, was a wire frame designed to support the large elephant's ears sprouting above the guests' heads. Keep in mind, however, that even on this large scale, intimacy at the dining level must be respected. As the guests sat down for dinner, they met the glow of small votive candles, which were square to echo the shape of the centerpiece base. It took some time to perfect the logistics of these types of creations, since they tend to be incredibly top-heavy. I have to admit that I've had to deal with my fair share of toppling centerpieces. (I once had a "tree of life" topple only seconds before a national TV appearance, taking down an expensive cake along with it!) These days, my staff and I are very careful to make sure the structure is completely sound before we even consider putting it out for any event. This time, I even went so far as to hang the largest ones from the ceiling to prevent any possible accidents. These fifteen-foot trees skimming the outskirts of the dining tables incorporated branches of Manzanillas draped with hand-sewn rose-petal wisteria flowers.

INSPIRATION FROM TROPICAL FRUITS
ECHOED AROUND THE ROOM, AND
*"pineapples" and "watermelons" and "bananas"
(right) highlighted the tables. The larger centerpieces (opposite) supported huge elephant's ears,
dwarfing guests under their canopy.*

These enormous sculptures took an amazing amount of time to construct, some up to eight hours with as many as five floral artists working at the same time. To build the pineapple, for example, pieces of foam were sculpted (with a handsaw) to form a perfect pineapple shape. Then wild green leaves were individually folded and pinned, overlapping onto the base. Thousands of miniature roses were hand pinned onto the pineapple-shaped foam core, and then double-checked to make sure that no petals were wilted or browning before the centerpiece was displayed.

At the bar, umbrella-like creations (opposite) of *flowing petals rained down from above in the warm colors celebrating the evening. This was the first time that anything like this had been brought into the bar, and the results were spectacular.*

One of the most important and instrumental elements of the entire reception was the lighting, beginning with the sunset-lit scrims for the cocktail hour. As dinner was served, the guests moved into the main dining room, which was (unbeknownst to them) equipped with "intelligent lighting," that is, lighting that can be controlled and can dramatically change the environment with the touch of a switch. As the evening progressed, the lighting slowly and almost imperceptibly changed from the muted blues of rain forest dusk to the darkness of a sultry evening. When the Latin band started the up-tempo dance music, bright lights punctuated the dance floor. As they played hours of salsa, rumba, and bolero music, the guests literally danced until dawn — again!

The cow sculpture (below) standing watch *over the seating cards took hundred of leaves and hours of time to construct. Haloed with a crown of orchids, it was the perfect combination of whimsy and elegance.*

A VIEW OF THE TROPICAL FIESTA (OVERLEAF).

Engaging Godiva Chocolate Fantasy

As I've said before, I love thinking outside the box in planning special events and their floral decor. But some of my most memorable creations had nothing to do with flowers at all, and one was actually derived from a gold box.

A couple recently came into my office to plan a surprise engagement party for their daughter — but they wanted something very unusual and different. The young man had asked for their daughter's hand in marriage during a winter carriage ride in Central Park, popping the question as she opened a box of Godiva® truffles, one of which he had replaced with a magnificent engagement ring. She was delighted and of course said yes! But her parents didn't want the fantasy to end there…They wanted to continue the theme at the party.

The fifty guests met at a loft in Manhattan, where they were introduced to one another and invited to mingle in the reception area, enjoy white chocolate martinis, and snack from the large chocolate-laden table set up in the main room. Arranged on the central table was a huge display of chocolate, in every variation imaginable, but that was just the beginning.

After the bride- and groom-to-be arrived — delighted to be surprised by family and friends — all were led into the main room for a luncheon. The room was luscious, decorated with golden hues and lined with six tables, each one sustaining a centerpiece overflowing with white and dark chocolate pieces. Even the boxes supporting the abundant displays were carved out of dark chocolate and resembled luxurious Christmas presents. The only inedible additions were sprigs of greens and pinecones, which added perfect textural contrast.

The walls were draped in a golden organza, and a wide ribbon circled the perimeter, as if the guests themselves were wrapped in the luxury of the signature Godiva box. Hanging on the walls were silk-screen panels, each a mouthwatering depiction of different chocolate pieces. The chairs were individually draped to resemble caramel pieces. For festive mood lighting, small votives filled with individually lit faux ice cubes were hung from the ceiling, which added a subtle complement to the warm russet-colored lighting.

What I loved about this small, intimate affair is that it highlighted how much you can use a single thing — in this case, chocolate — to create a one-of-a-kind fantasy with little or no dependence on flowers at all. A feeling of luscious abundance was reached using elements that were unusual and unique, tailored to the interests of the bride- and groom-to-be. Not only was it fun to design (after all, I love chocolate too), but it was a great lesson on thinking creatively and breaking the unwritten "rules" of special-event decor.

I DRAPED THE ENTIRE SPACE (LEFT)
IN THE SOFT, GOLDEN COLOR OF
the signature Godiva chocolate box — as well
as the seats — to literally surround guests at
the event. Adding gold lighting along the walls
finished the look.

FOR AN ADDED WHIMSICAL TOUCH OF
THE CANDY THEME, I PUT HANDMADE
twisted sugar sticks into each glass (overleaf, left),
which echoed the shape of the glass stems. Sterling-
silver antique sugar bowls contrasted nicely with
the golden surroundings.

SEMIOPAQUE PRINTED SCREENS (OVER-
LEAF, RIGHT) AROUND THE ROOM
artistically depicted pieces of chocolate. Lighting
them subtly from the back lent a romantic hue
to the room and added to the glowing golden feel.

Tender Oven Roasted Breast of Duck
Stuffed with Caramelized Onions
Warm Plum Sauce
Wild Rice Pilaf
with Julienne Vegetab...

Caramel No...

CHAPTER SIX

Beautiful Ballroom Fantasy

THE PLAZA HOTEL IS ONE OF THE MOST STATELY AND RECOGNIZABLE LANDMARKS IN NEW YORK — REMINISCENT OF A ROMANTIC French château, it regally surveys Central Park's southern entrances. I've designed several events here, and creating new and different ideas is always an exciting challenge. This 250-guest wedding was planned for early autumn — a striking time of year that is perfect for taking advantage of nature's own textures and colors.

The ceremony was held in the Rose Room — a beautiful space with floor-to-ceiling gold drapery on the windows. In the center of the room, I presented the only decor for the vows — a fifteen-foot-tall chuppah constructed entirely of fall foliage. Over an unfinished rustic wooden framework and wisteria vines I wove thousands of leaves that were just changed into the season's glorious colors of burgundy, orange, and maize. I used these natural and unstructured textures on the chuppah to contrast with the room's luxurious surroundings. It may seem like a strange design pairing; however, I found that the golds and oranges of the

leaves perfectly balanced with the royal tones of the room. The juxtaposition of the heavy curtains and lush carpeting with the organic statement of the chuppah created the perfect homage to the season, and subtle lighting at the base mimicked an evening sunset streaming through the boughs.

Guests moved into the Terrace Room for the cocktail hour, where I continued the seasonal impressions that were already introduced. I stayed away from repeating the autumn leaves in favor of something new. I designed two oversized arrangements of sunflowers, highlighted with pastoral terra-cotta pots and various fall-harvest fruits. Since sunflowers display a beautiful array of yellow and rusted-orange hues, they perfectly complemented the golden highlights in the room's architecture and added depth to the rustic pots that were used as foundations. Woven into the sculptures were apples, green and red grapes, and ripe plums — all of which supplemented the design's deference to the season's bounty. By creating only two large arrangements — each using hundreds of sunflower blooms — I avoided being overly ornamental or cluttered. White pillar candles surrounded the larger of the two and added a romantic glow.

When you make one or two strong central statements and there is ornate architecture in the room already, there's really no need to create any more dramatic elements. This is a perfect example of a case in which adding anything more to the ceremony

Each of the tall centerpieces on the reception tables was inspired by uniquely shaped glass vases (previous spread). This way, no two designs were exactly the same, yet the completed vision was cohesive and unified.

or cocktail decor would have merely been distracting, especially since the leaves and sunflowers already contributed a naturally unstructured feel. Keeping to one or two larger design elements is more than enough to communicate an idea to your company, and it is an easy rule to follow when planning your own event.

The reception was quite different in its style, and as guests entered the Grand Ballroom for the dinner reception, they left the rustic fall season behind them. They passed under a curtain of miniature Cymbidium orchids — each one individually threaded and hung from the frame of the door — and entered into a world sparkling with clear glass, brilliant whites, and pale greens. To set the tone, guests were greeted by a glorious all-white, five-tiered Sylvia Weinstock cake majestically standing by the door, embellished with thousands upon thousands of handmade flowers.

Each of the long dining tables hosted two large centerpieces. Resting on bases covered with hundreds of individually pinned orchids were tall, clear glass containers — each one a different shape. I used these oversized glass vases as inspiration for each centerpiece sculpture, treating each unique silhouette as its own piece of artwork. Some vases hosted winding vines of pale green miniature orchids climbing up their linear sides; others were adorned with circlets of white orchids around their curved midsections; and still others contained handmade wisteria, which hung gently inside. Each sculpture was crowned with a distinctive arrangement of hydrangea blooms and pale green orchids, and no two tables were exactly the same. Surrounding these sparkling creations were bowls that each contained a large floating rose, created with oversized white rose petals. On each guest's plate rested a gold napkin, adorned with a single large white orchid, and all was set on soft gold tablecloths that complemented the subtle gold accents in the room flawlessly.

Look around the room hosting your event and try to incorporate design elements in interesting places. In this case, we took to the walls, where oversized silk-screened vases were embellished with thousands of blooms (opposite). It appeared as though ornate period paintings encircling the guests were springing to life to join the celebration — a real fantasy-turned-reality.

The lofty ceiling space already hosted gorgeously detailed architecture and intricate molding, so I did not have to design any overhead pieces to fill the space. However, on the balconies overlooking the room, I introduced a popular Preston Bailey design — silk screens featuring traditional vases, each containing a three-dimensional arrangement of various flowers. Every panel was unique, and this luxurious addition made it seem as if the very artwork in the room were coming alive for the celebration. As a final but important touch, I added subtle gold lighting to lend an ethereal air to the event.

Ideas and visions don't always come easily when I meet with clients, and sometimes it takes a few missed cues before we hit the right direction. My initial sketches and presentations were completely incompatible with what the bride and groom wanted, and we went through a process of trial and error before we finalized the designs for

this event. My first presentation consisted of a white-hued ceremony and a deep, richly colored reception — not what they had in mind at all. The bride's mother is a successful interior designer with very specific taste, and since she was instrumental in the process, we worked very hard to cre-

ate the final vision together. My first efforts were too heavy-handed, and it took a few meetings to effectively communicate the style and sensitivity that they envisioned. They imagined a very graphic, textural statement, but still light and not overstated. In the end, ironically, we essentially swapped my initial ideas around, choosing a richly hued ceremony design and then moving into a fresh, clean, white backdrop with golden accents for the reception. It worked beautifully, and as a whole, created a story line of statements unlike anything I'd worked on before.

USING FRUIT (RIGHT) IS A WONDERFUL WAY TO ADD EARTHY COLORS AND *diverse textures to an event's design — and in general, seasonal fruits are conveniently found in complementary colors. The golden apples combined with the ripe red grapes and purple plums were the perfect addition to the bright sunflowers and continued the autumn-inspired feeling of abundance and bounty initiated in the ceremony's leaf-strewn chuppah.*

CHAPTER SEVEN

New England Waterfront Fantasy

SEPTEMBER IS ONE OF MY FAVORITE MONTHS FOR WEDDINGS. IT'S THE TIME OF YEAR WHEN YOU CAN STILL FEEL THE WARMTH OF summer, yet the cool touch of fall is in the air. The season is heavenly — a last-ditch effort from Mother Nature to impress us with warm and hazy conditions, often ushered in with a breeze, before settling into the hibernation of winter. Colors are an especially important consideration when planning events during this time of year. While it's a wonderful time to use bold, strong colors, it's important not to overstep the bounds of good taste and push too many colors into the mix. Keeping tones rich and bright without creating competition among them can be a challenge . . . but it can be so rewarding! And while September weather can be unpredictable in New England, we were fortunately graced with a picture-perfect day.

ENTRANCES CAN BE ONE
OF THE MOST STUNNING
*parts of the design (left
and opposite), so be sure you
pay them special attention.
Think of walkways not as a
means of getting from one place
to another, but as part of a continuing story line of the day.*

FANTASY WEDDINGS

{ 92 }

The wedding ceremony was held in a gorgeous white-steepled church in the green Connecticut countryside. For the aisle, we created twelve hydrangea-and-rose columns, attached them to several of the pews, and topped each one with a single tall taper. Two larger sculptures flanked the altar and were topped with five white pillar candles. The contrast of the white hydrangeas and green vines spiraling up the sides of the sculptures created a strong but romantic feel that did not compete with the church's surroundings and wooden accents.

As the bride entered, she passed beneath a glorious arch made of white hydrangeas and peach roses, which framed the dramatic commencement of the day perfectly.

This brings up an important point. When considering the decor for the special day, don't neglect entrances and walkways. For example, we wanted to create a statement that would help guests locate the site of the reception and that would catch their attention when they arrived. As I am not one to settle for the commonplace, I went with a hot-air balloon on the front lawn. Not only was the balloon colorful and festive, but it also lent quite an unexpected and fanciful touch to the event, transitioning perfectly from the wedding to the festive mood of the reception. This made a far more impressive statement than the expected mailbox decorations, and was a lively topic of conversation for the evening.

The cocktail hour and the reception dinner were hosted behind the bride's parents' home — cocktails took place outside, overlooking Long Island Sound on the shore of their property, and the reception was held in a large tent. In the backyard were several tables covered with ivory-and-pink checkered table-cloths. Muted pinks, greens, and cream oversized topiaries graced the tables as centerpieces. Each echoed the colors of the home's stonework and the informal French garden. A floral sculpted lion stood guard, made of thousands of open-faced roses, mounted atop a bold base of blue and green hydrangea clusters and rose accents. The lion was a fun and whimsical touch, I'll admit — but was not completely out of context in the setting. Looking straight ahead, the lion gazed at the crystal-clear September afternoon towards an unparalleled view of the Manhattan skyline in the distance.

Don't assume that every row in a church needs decoration. Sometimes a few dramatic statements — like these pillars of flowers (right) — are enough. It may be tempting to fill in every blank, but often these open spaces help enhance the displays you have.

The bride and groom made a stunning entrance, unlike anything I'd seen before. Since both the church and the bride's parents' estate sat on a pictur-esque shoreline, they decided to transport themselves to the reception via a small yacht. Their entrance could not have been timed more perfectly, and as the sun made a glorious and colorful exit on the horizon, the couple arrived at the dock, which was decorated with hanging flowers and faux butterflies.

The reception decor was very exciting to design, and I took inspiration from the couple's desire for something playful and strong inside the tent. The colors we used were a mixture of summer and fall tones, based on oranges and creams. In contrast to the floral accents, the tent walls were a draped blue fab-ric, mimicking the beautiful body of water outside. This gave a warm and invit-ing feeling to the 250 guests, and the deep color of the textile was the perfect backdrop to the pale linens and strong colors in the various arrangements around the room.

THE CREAMY AND VIBRANT COLORS (LEFT) OF THIS EVENT WERE INSPIRED *by the late summer–early fall season. A spotlight from above softly lit each table's centerpiece, making the various hues seem to radiate.*

THE SPARKLING GLOW OF CANDLELIGHT IS A WONDERFUL WAY TO ADD INTIMACY *and romance to the table settings (opposite). But when incorporated around the entire event space, the cumulative effect is a glowing, ethereal aura.*

THE CONTRASTING DRAPED BLUE FABRIC OF THE TENT ENHANCED THE RADIANCE *of the floral tints (overleaf). I consider the tent a canvas upon which designs can make an astounding appearance.*

Each table featured as a centerpiece a tall, clear glass flute overflowing with an abundance of orange, apricot, and ivory roses and orchids. Inside the flute hung a single, oversized hand-sewn wisteria accent, made of perfect cream-colored rose petals. The tablecloths were crisp white linen embroidered with a subtly beaded windowpane pattern. White pillar candles gave a strikingly romantic glow to each table, and reflected perfectly off the clear glassware and glass centerpieces. Each place setting had carefully folded napkins holding two perfect roses.

Hanging from the ceiling were six oversized gas-lantern-shaped sculptures, which introduced a very traditional shape to the event in a very untraditional way. The bride loved these in my initial sketches, and while I was originally planning on only one or two, she insisted that we put six of them above the dance floor. Made with sturdy wire framework, each was covered with an abundance of peach, orange, and cream flowers. Accented with tall pillar candles (electric, of course; see p. 116), they also helped to break up the blue drapery of the ceiling. The dance floor itself was inspired by an Aubusson carpet which we printed on vinyl and which echoed the color statements around the room.

The tent's main focus was a glorious five-tiered Sylvia Weinstock cake, placed in the center of the room on a round table draped in white silk. The all-white cake was accented with thousands of handmade flowers, and since the cake itself was so ornate,

THE GLORIOUS FIVE-
TIERED CAKE (OPPOSITE)
was placed near the center of the
room and made a particularly
dramatic central statement.
Made with thousands of flowers,
the cake itself was so spectacular
that it was set atop a very
simple, unadorned round table.

no further decoration was needed around it. I lit it with soft-edged spotlights from the ceiling to make it stand out and to give it a celestial presence.

This is the perfect example of an event that was decorated with the lush and radiant colors of the fall season, as well as with the light and airy colors of the departing summer, to create a tasteful balance of both seasons. It's

THE AUBUSSON-INSPIRED
DANCE FLOOR (ABOVE)
was created especially for this
event. It was a stunning addi-
tion to the overall feel of the
room and is a great example of
how historical touches can add a
unique flavor to your decor.

important to keep in mind that extravagant touches (like the hot-air balloon) can add excitement to any fantasy event, although too many can overwhelm guests. A profusion of colors and textures can be exquisite on their own — without any bells and whistles!

COULD YOU ASK FOR
A MORE BEAUTIFUL
evening for a wedding? This
gorgeous sunset (right) escorted
the newlyweds to the reception,
and while I know to never
depend on good weather, even
Mother Nature seemed to want
to celebrate the day.

STATIONED IN FRONT OF THE HOUSE,
THIS MAGNIFICENT HOT-AIR BALLOON
(left) was a beacon for guests arriving from the
chapel. I think it works better than a big bow on
the mailbox, don't you?

PINK-HUED TOPIARIES (OPPOSITE)
MADE WITH ROSES AND HYDRANGEAS
brought a stylistic garden touch to the cocktail
tables but didn't clash with the surrounding garden
and terrace decor. The stonework on the house
was a wonderful and stately background.

THE COLORFUL LION SCULPTURE (PREVIOUS
SPREAD), BUILT WITH HUNDREDS OF
roses, stood like a bright sentinel during backyard
cocktails. As you can see, even this whimsical
statement looks majestic and serene as it gazes
towards the horizon.

CHAPTER EIGHT

American Royalty Fantasy

WHEN A BRIDE-TO-BE CAME TO ME AND TOLD ME ABOUT HER FANTASY WEDDING, I KNEW WE WERE HEADED FOR A CELEBRATION fit for American royalty. But with a fantasy vision comes a certain challenge: how to take a unique opportunity to create larger-than-life settings but still remain tasteful. The bride wanted a bold statement, but we both agreed that we wanted to avoid looking "overdone." She knew she wanted grandeur, but paired with sophistication and dignity. She trusted my ability to find the right balance of these elements, and doing so proved to be an interesting challenge.

With five hundred guests on the invitation list, this midwinter wedding was truly a sight to behold. The formal nuptial ceremony was held in the opulent Grand Ballroom of the Waldorf-Astoria, where royalty worldwide have often celebrated special events. The decor needed to fit the striking interior and lavish surroundings but not overpower the affair. The end result was a surprisingly simple idea, using only roses that were sculpted into extraordinary statements that literally surrounded guests and bridal party alike.

The primary challenge for the ceremony was managing the height of the ballroom. Four stories high, the towering ceiling created a vast space that longed to be filled, and we needed something dramatic but elegant. Chandeliers have always been graceful

fillers of large spaces, so we created four huge floral "chandeliers" of petals, flowing down from the ceiling like multilayered water-falls. I hired a metalworker to create the four ten-foot in diameter and eight-foot in diameter rings, which were secured to the ceiling.

WHAT IS STATELIER THAN A WEDDING AT *the Waldorf-Astoria? The arched floral chuppah (above) displayed thousands of hand-placed roses in the Grand Ballroom of this historic hotel. Behind the bride and groom was a printed screen adorned with handmade wisteria accents.*

Using only white and cream roses, we threaded thousands of petals from the circular frames, allowing them to drape from the ceiling. The chandeliers filled the space with a look that was sculpted yet still maintained a light and airy touch of romance.

On the ground floor, the aisle was lined with twelve-foot constructed trees, adding a natural feel to the room. Birch tree limbs in white box bases were lushly adorned with box-wood evergreens and hanging flowers that were also created

THE MOST DRAMATIC STATEMENTS IN THE *Grand Ballroom were the four floral "chandeliers" (opposite and previous spread) that were suspended above the guests. Each construction was three stories high, elegantly displaying thousands of hand-strung white rose petals and filling the open space of the room.*

with thousands of rose petals. This dramatic yet slightly unstructured feel astounded the guests as they entered the room, and it formed a luxurious floral arch over the wedding procession.

THE GLORIOUS AISLE (LEFT) IS
REMINISCENT OF A STROLL THROUGH
*an idyllic garden. The slightly unstructured
trees — sporting thousands of hand-strung
white petals — graced the path and brought a
dreamlike quality to the procession.*

Time was another major factor, since we were permitted access to the ball-room only during the day of the ceremony. I pushed the rules as far as I could, and my crew arrived exactly at midnight and worked for sixteen hours straight — and we still were hurried in the end. But because of the limited time we had in the ballroom, preproduction was of the utmost importance for this event. We spent the week prior stringing petals onto the vast chandelier constructs and then storing them carefully in a cool, moist environment. This was truly an event where we had to rely on the hardiest of flowers.

The cream raw-silk runner had a subtle print design, reminiscent of a garden path. It led to the arched chuppah, which supported hundreds of rose-petal clusters that were suspended over the couple. The supporting posts were covered with evergreens and roses, and lit dramatically from the base to add to the heavenly feel. Loose petals scattered underfoot added the final touch to the perfect fantasy.

Since the wedding ceremony was such an abundant vision of creams and whites, we went in a completely different direction for the reception. As the reception was going to be held at another location — the Cipriani 42nd Street Ballroom — we agreed that it needed to be different while still maintaining the same level of taste and decorum. The contrast between the two events was felt most in the color scheme. While the wedding celebrated a profusion of white petals, the reception was a dramatic display of deep, passionate colors.

People are often afraid of using bold colors, but if you use them correctly and in the right situation, they can add a dimension as no other element can. The key is to refrain from using more than two or three complementary colors. Here we used reds and burgundies with touches of gold, which added a depth to the decor, making it feel warm and rich. It fit perfectly into the grand and lavish Cipriani Ballroom, and as the guests arrived from the ceremony, it made a welcome contrast to the cold winter weather outside.

For all of the floral elements at the reception, we used three components: orchids, roses, and berries. Even in the most ornate ideas we created for this celebration, the basic ingredients were surprisingly simple. My rule of thumb is to use only a few fundamental tools, and, with a bit of imagination, you can create incredibly elaborate arrangements. Once again, we were dealing with a vast

EACH TALL CENTERPIECE (ABOVE) RISES FROM A dense concentration of orchids and berries. When berries are combined with flowers in centerpieces — adding a wonderful contrast in texture — the colors must be complementary.

THE GRAND CHANDELIER SUSPENDED FROM THE ceiling (opposite) was decorated entirely with ribbons and hand-strung rose petals — a particularly romantic statement that also helped to visually fill the lofty ceiling space.

open space above the guests' heads. Since the chandelier worked so well in the Waldorf Ballroom, we were inspired to do the same for the reception. But this time we used ribbons and electric candles in addition to the rose petals. (Another important rule of thumb — whenever candles are used overhead, use electric candles. No matter how well the party is going, dripping hot wax on your guests is not a good idea — leave wax candles on the tables!)

Long rectangular tables were used to accommodate the large party, and they also allowed me to be creative with the centerpieces. Each table had two tall structures as well as a lower centerpiece between them. An urn sculpted with cranberries and orchids supported the taller pieces, which were composed of a profusion of roses, orchids, and draping floral clusters. A gold-wrapped

pole, spotted with cranberries, and originating from a base sculpted with Cymbidium orchids and more cranberries, held this all aloft. While we didn't use a huge variety of flowers, this is a perfect example of how contrasting textures can really make a dramatic statement.

The lower centerpieces were floral-covered boxes with orchids overflowing the top edges. All was set on a burgundy raw-silk underlay tablecloth with a sheer hand-beaded gold overlay — a perfect complement to the royal feel of the surrounding environment.

Lighting exaggerated what was already available, and was enhanced with the gold and burgundy touches around the room. Small clusters of votives warmed the table lighting, and added the soft glow of romance at a more intimate level.

It's important to note how simple the raw elements were. By using only one kind of flower for every structure in the entire ceremony ballroom, and only three for the reception, we managed to make both environments look completely unique and luxurious. Even the more complex structural elements, such as the chandeliers, were made using relatively simple fundamentals — the key was using them in dramatic and exceptional ways to create a distinct, one-of-a-kind statement for a wonderful, one-of-a-kind event.

CHAPTER NINE

Magnificent Mar-a-Lago Fantasy

INSPIRED BY MY FIRST BOOK, *DESIGN FOR ENTERTAINING*, A FLORIDA BRIDE CALLED ME AND HIRED ME OVER THE PHONE — BEFORE WE

even met in person. Since that was a remarkable leap of faith, I knew immediately that she had a distinct sense of style and would

be very involved in the creative process. From concept to reality, the designs for this wedding took nearly a year to complete, and

the bride and I went through several revisions before settling into our final presentations. But she had a remarkable eye, and work-

ing with her and her family was an exciting and enjoyable experience.

Set at the historic Mediterranean Revival mansion of Mar-a-Lago in Palm Beach, the wedding was in December, and the

bride wanted a winter-white ceremony. The reception, however, was full of lively colors. Both ceremony and reception were held

in massive tents constructed on the property. Spanish for "from sea to lake," Mar-a-Lago, a 118-acre property formerly owned by

Marjorie Post and now by Donald Trump, nestles between a lake and the pristine Atlantic shoreline — the perfect setting for a tented wedding and reception!

The three primary events — the ceremony, the cocktail hour, and the reception — all had their own style and were distinctively different in design and concept. However, it was important to maintain a consistent vision; the progression from one celebration to the next through the course of the evening had to remain seamless.

Entering the ceremony tent, the four hundred guests were greeted by a large white gate adorned with hundreds of hand-sewn petals and two large hydrangea arrangements. A boys' choir echoed through the lofty space, lending a holy and serene touch and welcoming guests to a spiritual oasis. The ceremony area was filled with a dozen birch-bark trees lining the aisle, adorned with thousands of leaves and sparkling with hundreds of individually hung votive candles. Each seat was draped with white fabric in keeping with the theme of the entire room. Red rose petals at each chair were the only flash of color, and also hinted at the rich colors of the reception to come.

When the bride was ready to enter, the ornate gate swung open slowly, and the lights around the room changed to a heavenly blue. The bride proceeded through the winter garden wonderland, down the aisle, and to the lit chuppah, which was designed to resemble a romantic garden gazebo and a floating sanctuary at the end of the petal-strewn and airy path to matrimony. As the bride and groom exited, guests celebrated by tossing colored rose petals.

During the cocktail hour, guests were invited to mingle around the pool cabanas and take informal tours through the historic 1927 mansion. Since the surrounding pool area and architecture were so beautiful, we decided to keep floral decor minimal. Seating assignments and escort cards were presented in rows — almost like tiny floral soldiers — each accompanied by a single floating gardenia and votive candles. Two large arrangements stood guard, made with white hydrangea, roses, and orchids streaming down the sides of tall, clear glass vases. The guests were delighted: they had a warm Florida evening perfect for outdoor cocktails, and the flexibility to walk around and explore the house before dinner began.

The reception's decor contrasted beautifully with the delicate feel of the ceremony and cocktail hour through the introduction of vibrant colors like reds and oranges. The tent was draped in taupe fabric — a perfect complement to the strong colors we were working with around the room. Each table was draped with rich, hand-brocaded tablecloths. The chairs were covered with organza fabric with beads dangling from the bottom to round out the lush feel at the tables.

Three types of centerpiece sculptures alternated at tables around the room: traditional floral topiaries, candelabras, and low centerpieces. All used the basic elements — bright reds and deep burgundies, accented with candles — but each was also unique.

Hanging from the draped ceiling were two major designs: a floral-infused old-fashioned lantern draped with petals, and a bell-shaped profusion of flowers made with hundreds of individually strung blooms. Using different yet complementary designs around the room — both on the tabletops and above guests' heads — gave the event more visual interest and variety, and offered me the opportunity to be creative with the space.

The dance floor was a printed copy of an Aubusson carpet motif. But we added our own whimsical touch: the bride and groom's new initials were incorporated into the ornate design. Framing the sides of the tent were my signature silk screens of oversized vases, enhanced with a wealth of flowers bursting from the walls.

Overall, the event felt traditional but not stuffy. We wanted guests to feel as though they were surrounded by an abundance of warm, passionate colors and textures, but not be overwhelmed by dark colors or heavy fabrics. To achieve this, we layered the textures, fabrics, and colors to achieve visual excitement.

The liveliness of the room was originally inspired by the surprise ending to the event — at midnight, World Music's most acclaimed artists, the Gipsy Kings, appeared and celebrated with a performance of their rumba flamenco music! With this in mind, the bride and I collaborated to create an environment that would be conducive to both a traditional wedding reception and a spicy serenade.

The event was a spectacular success, and the fusion of a variety of design elements flowed perfectly. From the angelic voices of a boys' choir echoing through the airy white tent before the ceremony to the vivacious and colorful environment of the reception, it was a perfect example of how very different visions can be used in harmony throughout a single evening. Keep this in mind when planning your own fantasy wedding — nothing is off limits as long as you work to keep a coherent progression and vision of the entire day's events.

THE AUBUSSON-STYLE FLOOR (PREVIOUS SPREAD) UNIFIED THE ENTIRE SPACE IN *color and style. I was quite relieved when it was laid out, since I hadn't been able to see the finished design until it arrived the day before the event.*

OVERSIZED FLORAL CANDELABRAS (OPPOSITE) SERVED AS IMPRESSIVE *centerpieces for select tables around the reception hall. When considering designs for centerpieces, keep in mind not only the overall room, but how guests will enjoy them while seated.*

INSPIRED BY ANTIQUE GAS LAMPS OF A BYGONE ERA (ABOVE), THESE *arrangements evoked a feeling of romantic nostalgia. But instead of wrought iron and glass, we used roses and hand-sewn rose-petal bunches, each individually attached to the wire framework underneath.*

THIS FLORAL "LAMPSHADE" (RIGHT) WAS A UNIQUE SCULPTURE, BUILT *with hundreds of petals and blooms. This was one of two ornate lamp designs hanging overhead; it took the bride and me a while to finalize the silhouettes. But once completed, they were exquisite.*

CANDLES ARE ALWAYS A WELCOME TOUCH TO A DINNER TABLE (OPPOSITE) *and add light without overwhelming guests. From votives to pillars, wax candles are gorgeous, but be sure that they are sitting securely in a base that can catch any stray drips. When using candles overhead, always stick to electric versions.*

THE TAUPE-COLORED DRAPED CEILING (ABOVE) WAS THE PERFECT BACKDROP *to the dramatic colors of the event. When working with the bold colors of the reception, I wanted a canvas that wasn't stark white, but also wouldn't get lost in the decor in the space. This perfectly surrounded the guests and highlighted the rich tones without feeling overdone.*

CHAPTER TEN

Signature Preston Bailey

I OFTEN ENVY FASHION DESIGNERS BECAUSE THEY COME OUT WITH NEW LINES EVERY SEASON. BUT AS I WAS WORKING ON AN EVENT last fall, I suddenly realized that I could approach my work in the same way. And from this thought I created my Signature line.

My goal in presenting this line is to allow you to take these designs and make them your own. From a minimalist ribbon-edged place mat in the "Blue Mood" collection to a luscious centerpiece sculpture in the "Textures" collection, each piece can stand alone or can be used in conjunction with others to make your personal vision a reality.

Each collection is inspired by colors and textures. Creative ideas come from a myriad of places and I encourage you to use the collections not as a dictation of what style should be, but instead as a launching point for getting your own concepts flowing. Think of all of these arrangements in various colors, combinations, and groupings — with each expressing its own unique style. Visualize the "Petal Fantasy" in off-white hues or the "Organic Architecture" collection in soft greens — these are the beginning of your own musings and thus, the blueprint for your event.

Like anyone in the design industry, I've learned much through trial and error over the years. Some designs I've loved and used in many different ways, and others were not as successful. The following pages are a collection of the designs that I love and have used again and again. I thrive when trying new things and am always pushing myself to find fresh and exciting directions. I want to bring that challenge and excitement to you as well, and I'm hoping that my enthusiasm will be contagious.

Petal Fantasy

A BRILLIANT FALL THEME, FULL OF RICH AUTUMN COLORS. RELYING HEAVILY ON orange and rust-colored blooms, it's accented by bright, plump berries. Providing soft accents around the walls of the room on a shimmering organza screen hang tiny votive candles (opposite), suspended at varying heights by ribbons.

THE INDIVIDUAL ELEMENTS ARE SCULPTED FROM THE SIMPLEST INGREDIENTS. The rose-petal centerpieces (right) — available in various sizes — are built by layering petal after petal around a central, luscious bud. The end result is a glorious oversize rose that floats in a living container, created with mini chrysanthemums. Under each clear charger plate, a petal-detailed place mat brings the look to each guest.

This "weeping willow" tree (opposite), created with individually strung petals and orchids, is a stately centerpiece. The fall colors are perfect for an evening event but can be reinterpreted in whites for a lighter daytime feel.

Cymbidium orchids float gracefully on a living container of mini chrysanthemums (above). Using these blooms individually or in larger clusters is a great way to vary the design but keep consistency.

Reinterpreted with kale leaves, this centerpiece uses lighter colors (right). I love the frilled texture of the kale leaves' soft green hues with lavender accents. The smaller arrangements are made with pristine white rose petals, and highlighted with brunia berries.

Blue Mood

THE CASCADING PETALS OF THIS CENTERPIECE *(opposite) create a favorite shape of mine. Each stream is tipped with a delicate orchid suspended gently above the guests. This is a wonderful way to provide a dramatic statement for the room without visually obstructing an intimate brunch or dinner conversation.*

FROSTED-GLASS CONTAINERS DISPLAY THE RIBBON ACCENT IN A SOFT, *delicate way. The fingerbowls float hydrangea florettes in complementary blue hues. There are layers upon layers of flowers — a fabulous way to take simple elements and bring depth and dimension to a look.*

THE WHITE LINEN HAND-STITCHED NAPKINS KEEP WITH THE "BLUE MOOD" *with more double-faced satin ribbon (left) and accented with tiny hydrangea details. The place mat integrates successfully with the delicate ribbon edging. Available in different hues, this theme can be reinterpreted in everything from pale shades to rich, bold colors, each one evoking its own emotion.*

REPEATING SHAPES IN DIFFERENT SIZES, THESE FROSTED GLASS VASES *(right) sport small, medium, and large clusters of hydrangeas. Notice how the details on the glass are slightly different, yet blend together wonderfully.*

EXPERIMENT BY USING DIFFERENT YET COMPLEMENTARY BLOOMS, LIKE *these variegated blue-and-white hydrangeas in the forefront paired with the bold, white lisianthus in the background (below).*

INSPIRED BY RENOWNED DESIGNER VICENTE WOLF, THIS COLLECTION IS *motivated by the unique style of this brilliant interior designer. The cool, glacier-blue hues are amazingly romantic and soft. The dramatic lanternlike centerpieces (opposite) are detailed with petals and gracefully suspend ribbon-accented containers of votive candles. The French satin double-faced ribbons are echoed on the panels in the background — which is a unique way of displaying seating assignments for your guests.*

Warm and Sultry

A COLLECTION INSPIRED BY CURVA-
CEOUS FEMININE FORM AND LINE.
*The shapely, clear hourglass vase supporting the
dramatic centerpiece (opposite) was the inspiration
for the collection, and the profusion of deep-hued
flowers brings the look to a dramatic head.*

SUSPENDED IN THE INTERIOR SPACE
OF THE VASE IS A HAND-SEWN ROSE-
*petal creation built with hundreds of individual
petals (left). Hanging gently inside the sinuous
form, this adds a subtle but unexpected element to
the tall container. This is one of my favorite looks
for clear glass — putting florals inside — which
can really add depth to the overall look.*

AT THE BASE OF THE CENTERPIECE
SCULPTURE (RIGHT), INDIVIDUALLY
*folded lemon leaves lend a pleated feel and are
accented with bright, ripe berries. The deep
green of the leaves adds a gorgeous contrast to
the rich colors in the collection and complement
the look perfectly.*

The silk screen (left) depicts a traditional ornate French *porcelain bowl, but it is brought to life with hundreds of floral blooms in deep hues. This is one of my signature designs. and one of the most dramatic. The decorative piece adds decor to the walls of a room in an unexpected way.*

When creating grand statements— like the hourglass vase (opposite) *and the printed screen (above) — adding details on the table level will maintain balance. The small, floating roses are a great touch, and combining them with small votive candles provides a very intimate feeling.*

Orchids (right) are one of the most versatile blooms, and they *come in hundreds of colors. sizes, and shapes. Just browsing the flower markets early in the morning is a fabulous way to get inspiration for your event. and individual blooms placed on guests' napkins is a favorite touch.*

THE DETAILING OF THE SILK SCREEN
IS EXQUISITE, AND I'VE CREATED THESE
screens in various styles and shapes. The French-
inspired bowl (right) is just one of many designs
that I've used, and it can be paired with different
blooms and colors for completely different looks.

THIS INTENSELY LAYERED LIVING
CONTAINER (BELOW AND OPPOSITE) IS
one of the most romantic and luscious statements
I've ever created. It is made using alluring roses
and calla lilies, and the sensual shapes and textures
of these two flowers complement each other exquis-
itely. Mixing up textures is a wonderful way to
vary designs and add a uniqueness to your own
individual statement.

Beyond Candles and Roses

TWO OF THE MOST FUNDAMENTALLY ROMANTIC ITEMS — CANDLES AND roses — are reinterpreted and taken a step further (opposite). These everyday elements are often used for weddings and special events, but in this collection, I challenged myself to take them in an unexpected direction.

EACH DISPLAY CONSISTS OF HANDMADE CANDLES, CUSTOM-SHAPED TO FORM various silhouettes. Sculpted with baby pink miniature roses (opposite below) and seated on a bed of magnolia leaves, the candles present a striking yet balanced juxtaposition of colors. The single candle seems to glow from a bed of soft rose petals — I can't imagine anything more sensual.

ENCIRCLED WITH AN ACCENT OF EUCALYPTUS SEEDS (ABOVE), THE flames from the candles softly heat the seeds and their heavenly scent drifts around the room.

THE CENTRAL CANDLES GLOW AS THEY FLOAT ON A BED OF PINK AND purple miniature roses (left). This collection of centerpieces is the perfect example of taking the expected and carving it into innovative formations. Twisting the simplest elements of romance — the candle and the rose — a singular, theatrical statement is made with this collection.

THIS GEOMETRIC-INSPIRED COLLECTION ENTHUSIASTICALLY CELEBRATES SHAPES *and forms and reinterprets them using a surprising variety of textures. The ovoid hanging sculptures (opposite) juxtapose a wire framework with delicate lacework of dried leaves. Gold and amber colors are highlighted with the sparkle of votive candles circling the rims.*

THE CENTERPIECE BASE AND SMALL PILLAR CANDLES (ABOVE) ARE WRAPPED *with amber-hued filigree leaves, bringing the overhead textures to an intimate level at the table. The warm glow of the candles accents the amber, gold, and cream blooms (right) perfectly. The shapes of the candles, centerpiece, and table echo the rounded forms overhead.*

Taking the geometric theme a step further, I've replaced the center *floral arrangements with sculpted handmade candles (left). We discovered this unique shape by putting two candles together, one on top of the other, and voilà — a new and unusual twist to a traditional element.*

The amber and golden colors (opposite) are warm and inviting — *a great look for an autumn or winter event. Softening the lines of the candles are bowls of floating white blooms at each place setting.*

I love the rounded shapes of the overhead sculptures (right). When *using large statements like these, organic touches — like berries and desiccated leaves — make them light and airy. Votives complete the mood, but be sure when using candles overhead that they are secure enough to avoid dripping wax on the table below. Better yet, use electric candles.*

Autumn Feast

THIS COLLECTION ENCOMPASSES A
DISTINCTLY ALL-AMERICAN FEELING OF
Thanksgiving abundance and is reminiscent of a
celebratory fall festival. I love the plentiful feel of
an overflowing bounty of flowers and fruits, and
a small cluster of both cover the base of the tall.
clear glass flute (opposite).

USING RIPE FRUITS COMBINED WITH
ORANGE AND AMBER-HUED FLORAL
accents (right). this is a modern interpretation of
a cornucopia. Grapes, apricots, and plums are
accented with roses and cymbidium orchids, layer-
ing the collection with a lush variety of shapes.

RIPE KUMQUATS ARE PERCHED ATOP
A RICH AMBER-COLORED BIOT GLASS
*(opposite), looking almost like a kumquat
cocktail. A symbol of good luck in certain cultures,
the rounded shapes form an aromatic bouquet and
work beautifully with the fertile tone of the room.*

THE FAWN-COLORED NAPKINS ARE
PRESENTED WITH THE CHEERFUL PLANT
*Japanese lanterns (above). I love this shape and the
lighter-than-air pillow-like feel of these dried flowers.
The place settings sit on a layer of desiccated
leaves, and the filigreed edges look like delicate
lace, yet still maintain an autumnal feel.*

DARK-PIGMENTED TRIANGULAR PILLAR
CANDLES (RIGHT) ARE STRIKING AND
*add a remarkable depth of tone to the table.
By using various elements of this collection —
combined with your imagination — you can create
your own vision of celebratory abundance.*

Organic Architecture

This architecturally inspired collection takes form and shape *to another level. Fields of celadon-hued hydrangea florettes and cinnamon stick details are individually applied to various surfaces (opposite), from Styrofoam bases making up the wall hangings, to candle edges, and even to place mats.*

The square shapes of this collection (right and below) are wonderfully *interchangeable and can be built upon to form many unique and different looks. The combination of various floral elements, hand-molded candles, and rustic and aromatic cinnamon sticks adds modern elegance to any type of special event.*

THINK BEYOND THE TABLES — AND ONTO THE WALLS. DECOR FOR ANY event shouldn't be limited to centerpieces but can be incorporated in innovative and creative places. With this repetition of floral "art" on the wall (above) — suspended gently by ribbons — we've really enveloped the room with a cohesive design statement.

ADDING CANDLES IS A SIMPLE YET STUNNING TOUCH (LEFT). Small, square votives add an element of romance and follow the linear shapes of the entire collection.

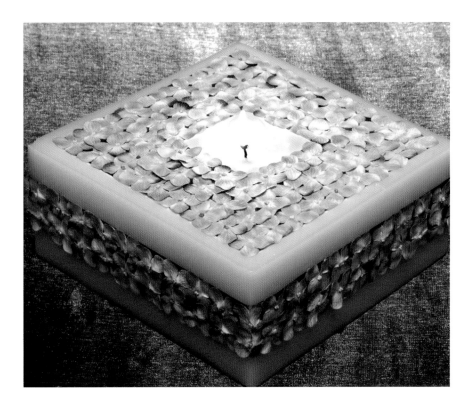

WHO SAYS CANDLES HAVE TO STAND ALONE? BY INCORPORATING HANDMADE candles into the floral designs (left), we've combined two elements into one centerpiece. Notice. however. that this also reflects the square outline of the over-all organic architecture theme.

OUR ARCHITECTURAL INSPIRATION DOESN'T STOP WITH CANDLES AND hydrangeas. and here we've incorporated other blooms into the mix. Miniature mums and orchids are built into the framework (below), introducing new organic textures to this collection. This is the perfect example of how effective repetition of shape can be.

Ethereal Elegance

THE ULTIMATE IN EXQUISITE ROMANCE, THIS COLLECTION EPITOMIZES THE *delicate style reminiscent of a dream. The white Phalaenopsis orchids (opposite) in the tall centerpiece are an abundance of perfect blooms that seem to float effortlessly above the table.*

ORCHID SHAPES ARE REPEATED ON VARIOUS LEVELS, EVEN DOWN TO THE *silver salt and pepper cellars (right) and candlestick holders. Echoing the dramatic shapes of the florals above, the metallic texture adds a new dimension. White peonies floating in clear glass containers add the perfect accent at an intimate level.*

AN OFT-NEGLECTED DECORATIVE OPPORTUNITY: CHAIRS AROUND THE room. *These covers (above) are a dramatic way to add a heavenly touch. On the left, sheer silver organza is embroidered with iridescent beading and metallic thread. In the middle is a glorious patch-work of pearl and organza, and on the right, sheer organdy with rosette details completes the trio.*

A WHITE PEONY AT ITS ABSOLUTE PEAK (RIGHT) SITS UNADORNED IN A CLEAR glass container. *When you have a single flower encompassing such perfection and beauty, why adorn it with unnecessary clutter and furnishings? Sometimes the simplest elements are the most exquisite, and by displaying them without distractions, you can achieve the maximum impact.*

Champagne and Caviar Dreams

INSPIRED BY SPARKLING CHAMPAGNE
AND CAVIAR, THE CRYSTALLINE TOUCHES
*in this collection are echoed in the overhanging
vases, candle votives, and even the tablecloths with
payette details. The passionate colors and textures
in these designs complement the luxurious decor of
the Tiffany Suite at the St. Regis Hotel in New York,
where this formal engagement party was held.*

Tabletops display decadent quantities of champagne and *caviar in beaded and crystal-encrusted containers (opposite). The cool greens of the lady slipper orchids and miniature mums are the perfect accompaniment to the shimmering, delicate tablecloths.*

Each guest at the party received a personalized gift bag containing *luxurious caviar and miniature bottles of champagne. What better way to celebrate that special day?*

Centerpieces reminiscent of bridal bouquets (right) are a stunning *presentation — without water or vases — and hint at the impending nuptials. This is a fabulous way to think outside the box, and the single design serves two functions.*

BEAUTIFUL INVITATIONS SET THE
TONE FOR WHAT IS TO COME ON THE
wedding day. Invitation design by Lehr & Black
for Diane Setchen from Fancy That.

ACKNOWLEDGMENTS

There are so many people who have traveled this fantastical journey with me, and to whom I owe an overwhelming debt of gratitude. Several people, however, merit special mention and my deepest thanks:

Jill Cohen, my publisher, whose unflagging commitment and enthusiasm for this book made it a reality. Kristen Schilo, my editor, whose attention to detail and coordination of my creative impulses were incalculable assets. Beth Decker, my writer, has been so wonderful. Photographer John Labbé's brilliant eye caught exquisite beauty in every shot.

My literary agent, Karen Gantz Zahler, is a most trusted colleague. The art director of this book, Lynne Yeamans, graced every page with her artful guidance and gave these fantasies an incredible life of their own.

Special thanks to my friends and colleagues who stayed the course with me through thick and thin: Bill Ash, for his extraordinary camaraderie; Sylvia Weinstock, colleague and mentor; Marcy Blum, friend and trusted advisor; and Elizabeth K. Allen, a truly amazing person with whom I've shared so much. A special thank you to Arthur Bacall and Harriet Rose Katz for unwavering companionship. My sincere appreciation to Jennifer Zabinsky and Claudia Hanlin at the Wedding Library. Also to my wonderful friend and planner, Judy Schwartz.

Special recognition is due to Sean Low, the president of my company, who offers tremendous and constant support to me; Bentley Meeker, who is truly a lighting genius and an extraordinary friend; Dara Wishingrad, my art director; and Michael Speir, who is an astonishing graphic designer.

Also, my sincerest thanks to my clients and friends who have supported and participated in the creation of this book and so much more in my life: Arte Italica, Creative Engineers, Peter Callahan Caterers, Frank Salaris of Frank Alexander NYC for his wonderful draping, the Ezrattis, the Friedmans, the Hahns, the Keidans, the Lavynes, the Levines, Liora Lights, the Nahmads, the Rennerts, Herb Rose, Lynn Schlereth, the Sterns, the Suhlers, Cipriani 42nd, the Pierre Hotel, the St. Regis Hotel, and Power House at the Natural History Museum.

BOTTOM ROW: LEFT TO RIGHT   *Elizabeth Iverson, office manager and assistant to Preston Bailey; Bill Ash, director of Signature Preston Bailey; Sanaw Ledrod, our most extraordinary head floral designer; Angkhana Chermsirivatana, floral designer; Eduardo Martins, production manager; Michelle Gannello, production designer and coordinator*

TOP ROW: LEFT TO RIGHT   *Oscar Simeon Jr., floral designer; Thomas Cawley, floral production and operations manager; Pedro Santos, assistant production manager; Sean Low, president, Preston Bailey Entertainment & Set Design; Luiz Fernando Leite, director of production and operations; Nadine Jervis, associate director of Signature Preston Bailey; Carlos Belo Jr., transportation; Olivia St. Louis, Preston Bailey Accounting; Anne Crenshaw, controller*